DATE DUE

UNITED STATES
SUPREME COURT
LIBRARY

Ruth Bader Ginsburg

by Bob Italia

ABDO & Daughters
Minneapolis, MN

Published by Abdo & Daughters, 4940 Viking Drive, Suite 622, Edina, Minnesota 55435.

Library bound edition distributed by Rockbottom Books, Pentagon Tower, P.O. Box 36036, Minneapolis, Minnesota 55435. International copyrights reserved in all countries. No part of this book may be reproduced in any form without written permission from the publisher. Printed in the United States.

Cover Photo: Archive Photos
Interior Photos: Wideworld Photos

Edited By Julie Berg

Library of Congress Cataloging-in-Publication Data

Italia, Robert, 1955-
    Ruth Bader Ginsburg / by Bob Italia
    p. cm. — (Supreme Court justices)
    Includes index and glossary.
    ISBN: 1-56239-098-8
    1. Ginsburg, Ruth Bader — Juvenile Literature. 2. Judges—United
States—Biography—Juvenile Literature. [1. Ginsburg, Ruth Bader.
2. Judges. 3. United States. Supreme Court—Biography.
4. Women --Biography.]
    I. Title. II Series.
        KF8745.G56I83   1994
        347.73'2634—dc20
        [B]
        [347.3073534]
        [B]
                                93-42168
                                    CIP
                                    AC

Table of Contents

A Historical Event

*I*t was a solemn ceremony. But the new U.S. Supreme Court Justice smiled as she made history. Family, friends, and dignitaries filled every seat in the courtroom.

Ruth Bader Ginsburg, the 107th Supreme Court Judge.

Almost unnoticed, a small woman entered without fanfare on the arm of the deputy clerk of court. She took her seat at a table down front. Ruth Bader Ginsburg was ready for her formal swearing-in to a Supreme Court that for the first time in history would have two women justices.

Ginsburg sat there as a silence took over the courtroom. Suddenly—*crack!*—down came the gavel of court marshal Alfred Wong, announcing the arrival of President Clinton, who chose Ginsburg for the court. But on this day he was just another spectator.

The president, after all, is the head of the executive branch of the United States government. This was the judicial branch's show.

Crack! The gavel struck again. Wong announced the arrival of the justices. "Oyez, oyez, oyez," he called out. "God save the United States and the honorable court."

The rest of the justices appeared at the high wooden bench in their black robes.

President Clinton looks on as Chief Justice Rehnquist helps the newest member of the Court, Ruth Bader Ginsburg, sign the Court's oath card.

After Attorney General Janet Reno presented Ginsburg to the court, the clerk led her up to Chief Justice William Rehnquist. She took her oath, looking out over the audience and smiling again as she pledged to "do equal right to the poor and to the rich." And then, grinning, she sat in the new justice's spot on the far right of the bench.

That was it. The ceremony took just six minutes.

Ginsburg then made an appearance for photos in the huge marble plaza in front of the court building. Rehnquist escorted her down the steps and then left her there. Eventually, her family joined her— children, grandchildren, mother-in-law and finally her husband.

Ginsburg made no formal statement. However, when sworn in at the White House in August 1993, she spoke of breaking down the traditional male dominance of the judiciary.

"I have no doubt," she said, "that women, like persons of different racial groups and ethnic origins, contribute ... a distinctive medley of views influenced by differences in biology, cultural impact and life experience."

Jane Ginsburg, daughter of Ruth Bader Ginsburg.

The Girl from Brooklyn

*R*uth Joan Bader Ginsburg was born in New York City on March 15, 1933. She grew up in a small but tidy two-story attached house on East Ninth Street. As a child, Ginsburg attended Public School 238 and James Madison High School in New York City.

At James Madison, Ginsburg was listed on the rolls of Arista, an honor society. She also served as treasurer of the Go-Getters, a pep rally club, and secretary to the English department chairperson. In addition, she was a member of the school orchestra, and an editor of the school newspaper.

Ginsburg received her undergraduate degree from Cornell University in Ithaca, New York. There she majored in government. She married fellow student Martin D. Ginsburg in 1954, the same year she completed her Bachelor of Arts degree.

RUTH BADER
1584 East 9th Street
Arista, Treas. of Go-Getters, School
Orchestra, Twirlers, Sec. to English
Department Chairman, Feature Ed-
itor Term Newspaper
Cornell University

**Ruth Bader Ginsburg's yearbook photo
from James Madison High School in New
York City.**

Ginsburg attended Harvard University Law School (1956-58) and was elected to the Harvard Law Review. She had been one of only nine women law students in her class. She remembered "wanting to drop through a trapdoor" when the dean at Harvard asked her to justify taking the place where a man could be.

After her husband took a job in New York City, she transferred to Columbia Law School.

At the White House in 1993, Ginsburg spoke of breaking down the traditional male-dominated judicial system.

Discrimination

*I*n 1959, Ruth Bader Ginsburg was about to graduate from Columbia Law School. Still, she was surprised that being on law review at both Harvard and Columbia and first in her class at Columbia did not make her a sought-after recruit. "Not a single law firm in the entire city of New York bid for my employment," she recalled. (She received LL.B. and J.D. degrees in 1959.)

Even worse, Supreme Court Justice Felix Frankfurter in 1960 declined to employ her as a clerk. He said he was not ready to hire a woman.

Ginsburg worked as a clerk for U.S. District Judge Edmund L. Palmieri from 1959 to 1961. She taught at Rutgers University Law School from 1963 to 1972 and at Columbia School of Law from 1972 to 1980. Teaching constitutional law and procedures, she became Columbia's first female-tenured professor.

Fighting for Equal Rights

*I*n the late 1960s and early 1970s, Ginsburg also acted as director of the Women's Rights Project of the American Civil Liberties Union. Between 1973 and 1976, she argued six cases on gender equality before the Supreme Court. Winning five of the six cases, she established legal grounds for

Ginsburg in 1957 at Harvard Law School, working for a U.S. Court of Appeals judge.

women's equality to men, among them *Frontiero v. Richardson* (1973) and *Craig v. Boren* (1976).

In the *Frontiero* case, she convinced the high court that rules regarding dependent-housing allowances in the military should be applied equally to servicemen and servicewomen. She also defended the principle of gender equality even when women had benefited from a law and, in doing so, inspired the high court to redefine its guidelines for gender-based laws.

15

Ginsburg views a display of George Washington's 1789 nominations to the first Supreme Court during a tour of the National Archives in Washington, D.C.

Ginsburg is shown a special women's
panel erected in her honor at Columbia
Law School in New York City. The panel is
for her work in sexual discrimination
cases.

In the 1976 case, she represented men and argued that an Oklahoma law allowing women, but not men, to purchase low-alcohol beer at the age of 18 was unconstitutional. Many observers compared her to the late Supreme Court Justice Thurgood Marshall. (As an attorney, Marshall had advanced civil rights for blacks through the legal system.)

Another of her cases successfully challenged a New Jersey regulation requiring pregnant teachers to quit without any right to return to the classroom. Ginsburg herself was forced to fake her way through her second pregnancy at Rutgers by wearing clothes one size too large during the spring semester. She gave birth in the early fall before classes resumed. Rutgers gave her tenure in 1969.

In 1971, Harvard, which had decided it was time to consider adding a female to the faculty, hired Ginsburg to teach a course on women and the law. When she did not receive a full-time offer a year later, she quietly packed her bags. She was not unemployed long. In 1972, Columbia Law School hired her as its first tenured female faculty member.

Martin & Family

Meanwhile, Ruth's husband Martin was on his way to becoming one of the top tax lawyers in the country. During Ruth's first semester at Cornell, Martin had given a lift to a friend in his old Chevrolet to pick up a date who lived in the dorm room next to Ginsburg's. That's how she met Martin. The minute Ruth graduated in 1954, they were married at the Ginsburg family home.

Martin served two years in the Army at Fort Sill, Oklahoma. There, the couple had their first meal cooked by Ginsburg. The tuna casserole was, Martin recalled, "as close to inedible as food could be." He started studying French cookbooks and became as fine a cook as he is an attorney.

When they got back to Harvard, the couple shared child care duties. They took turns relieving the babysitter every afternoon at 4:00. That began their lifelong practice of working well into the early morning hours.

Martin Ginsburg, husband of Supreme Court judge Ruth Bader Ginsburg.

Judge Ginsburg

*I*n 1980, President Jimmy Carter nominated Ginsburg to be a judge on the U.S. Court of Appeals for the District of Columbia Circuit. During her years as a federal judge, Ginsburg kept a moderate legal view. A 1988 study conducted by the *Legal Times* found that Ginsburg had sided more often with her colleagues on the federal bench who had been appointed by Republican presidents than with their Democratic counterparts. Ginsburg was selected as a judge inpart because of the national acclaim she received as counsel to the American Civil Liberties Union.

By the 1990s, Ginsburg had come to seem like a symbol of an earlier age to the younger women lawyers who now make up 2,496 of the total profession.

Supreme Court Nominee

*O*n June 14, 1993, President Clinton nominated Ruth Bader Ginsburg to replace retiring Justice Byron R. White on the Supreme Court.

The announcement capped an almost three-month search for a new Supreme Court justice, the longest in history. The president said that the White House had reviewed the qualifications of more than 40 potential candidates. These included Interior Secretary Bruce Babbitt

Supreme Court nominee Judge Ginsburg works in her Washington office.

and Judge Stephen G. Breyer of the U.S. Court of Appeals for the First Circuit in Boston.

The only other person the president had publicly mentioned as a possible Supreme Court justice was New York Gov. Mario M. Cuomo. But Cuomo withdrew from consideration in April 1993.

Regarding White's replacement, Clinton had said he would appoint a justice with "a fine mind, good judgment, wide experience in the law and the problems of real people, and someone with a big heart."

Ginsburg's nomination was the first time a Democratic president had named a Supreme Court justice since 1967. In his June 14 speech announcing the nomination, Clinton said he chose Ginsburg because she had proved to be wise and fair during her years of service on the federal bench. He described Ginsburg's legal work representing women's rights before becoming a judge as a "truly historical record of achievement."

Ginsburg, the president added, "cannot be called a liberal or a conservative. She has proved herself too thoughtful for such labels." Despite having a background in women's rights, Ginsburg was widely seen as a moderate. She was also a detail-oriented professional whose rulings on the District of Columbia Court of Appeals reveal neither conservative or radical views.

On June 14, Ginsburg heralded her nomination "because it contributes to the end of the days when women, at least half the talent pool in our society, appear in high places only as one-at-a-time performers."

In a statement that clearly moved the president, Ginsburg paid tribute to her late mother, saying, "I pray that I may be all that she would have been had she lived in an age when women could aspire and achieve and daughters are cherished as much as sons."

Ginsburg did not expand on her specific judicial views. But she said she was guided by the words of Chief Justice William H. Rehnquist regarding a judge's obligation to act fairly "even when the decision is not. . . what the home crowd wants."

Ruth Bader Ginsburg's nomination was expected to sail through the Senate. But there were concerns among liberals about the moderate position she had assumed on the Appeals Court (she has voted as often with the Republican appointees as with the Carter appointees). Women's groups are also worried over criticism the pro-choice Ginsburg leveled at the *Roe v. Wade* decision in a speech at New York University's School of Law in March 1993.

Roe v. Wade was the Supreme Court decision that had legalized abortion. Ginsburg had suggested that abortion rights should have been based on the issue of women's economic equality rather than on a right to privacy, as was established by the Court. Also, Ginsburg said that the Supreme Court should have legalized abortion bit by bit, rather than a sweeping manner.

Before the Senate

On July 29, 1993, the Senate Judiciary Committee unanimously endorsed the nomination of Judge Ruth Bader Ginsburg to sit on the Supreme Court. The full Senate was expected to vote on President Clinton's nominee before its early-August recess and confirmation was widely expected.

Committee Chairman Joseph Biden hailed Ginsburg as "the right choice" for the Supreme Court opening, and Senator William Cohen said that the judge had displayed "impeccable" character.

But the endorsement did not come easily. From July 20 to July 23, Judge Ginsburg fielded questions posed by the 18-member Judiciary Committee on a wide range of issues. Those issues included abortion, capital punishment and the role of the courts.

July 20, 1993, Judge Ruth Bader Ginsburg had her Senate Judiciary confirmation hearing on Capitol Hill. Here she poses with members of the Senate.

Ginsburg defined her view that the courts should play a nonactivist role in the formation of the law. But she also said that the courts should voice an opinion on social issues "when political avenues become dead-end streets." She freely discussed her previous legal rulings and writing, but generally stuck to a pledge of "no hints, no forecasts, no previews" of how she might decide particular cases that came before the high court.

Ginsburg strongly supported a woman's right to have an abortion, describing it as "something central to a woman's life, to her dignity." She also said that she believed abortion to be a fundamental right protected by the equal protection clause of the 14th Amendment.

Ginsburg was asked to discuss her views about bias-based on sexual orientation. She said, "I think rank discrimination against anyone is against the tradition of the U.S. and is to be deplored."

She did not answer direct questions whether she considered the death penalty to be unconstitutional. She noted that she had not written extensively on the subject.

Several senators criticized Ginsburg for failing to disclose a gift of membership from an exclusive country club. But they also said that it would not interfere with their decision to confirm her. Ginsburg joined the club which had traditionally waived its $25,000 initiation fee for federal judges. Later she resigned after it rescinded its fee waiver. She said that the club's move seemed to discriminate against one of her colleagues on the federal bench who could not afford the fee and happened to be black.

The proceedings were civil, in contrast to the 1991 confirmation hearings of Supreme Court Justice Clarence Thomas. (Thomas had been accused of sexual harassment by law professor Anita Hill.)

Following criticism that the then-exclusively male committee had mistreated Hill, two newly elected women senators, Diane Feinstein and Carol Moseley-Braun, had been placed on the committee.

Another change after the Thomas hearings was a private session to allow the airing of any sensitive information regarding a nominee. On July 23, 1993, the committee held its closed session with Ginsburg. But no new information was reportedly uncovered. Biden said the closed session would become standard practice for Supreme Court nominees.

Only Senator Jesse Helms spoke out against the nominee. Helms criticized Ginsburg's support for abortion rights. Conservative Republican Senators Don Nickles and Robert Smith joined Helms in voting against Ginsburg's confirmation.

In the wake of her Senate approval, lawmakers and officials hailed the smoothness of Ginsburg's confirmation proceedings as well as her judicial qualifications. Senator Joseph Biden, the chairman of the Senate Judiciary Committee, called Clinton's choice of Ginsburg "wise and insightful."

**Supreme Court Justice Ruth Bader Ginsburg
takes the oath to defend the Constitution in a
ceremony in the East Room of the White House
on August 10, 1993.**

Confirmation

*O*n August 3, 1993, the Senate voted 96-3 to confirm President Clinton's appointment of Judge Ruth Bader Ginsburg to the Supreme Court. Ginsburg succeeded Justice Byron White, who retired from the high court in June.

Upon her swearing in, Ginsburg became the 107th justice and the second woman to join the Supreme Court. (The first was current Justice Sandra Day O'Connor.) She was the first nominee of a Democratic president to be confirmed since Thurgood Marshall, a nominee of Lyndon Johnson, in 1967.

Ginsburg is the wealthiest justice on the high court. (She and husband Martin Ginsburg had a net worth of $6.1 million, according to financial documents released by the Senate Judiciary Committee July 6, 1993.) And she is the first Jewish justice since the resignation of Abe Fortas in 1969.

Ginsburg's Private Side

*F*or millionaires, the Ginsburgs live a simple life. They drive a six-year-old Nissan and a one-year-old Volvo. And, unlike most wealthy people, they don't have another house in the country.

For relaxation, Ginsburg enjoys the opera. She also likes to travel—whenever her busy schedule allows it. Ginsburg plays golf at the Army and Navy Club and a nearby Virginia resort. And she likes to water ski. Forty years later, Martin is still cooking— for friends at the couple's duplex apartment at the Watergate in Washington, D.C.

The Ginsburgs' oldest child, Jane, 37, is following her mother's footsteps by teaching law at Columbia. Son James, 27, is attending law school while producing classical records in Chicago.

What the Future May Bring

Although a leading figure in the legal fight for gender equality, Ruth Ginsburg was expected to bring a complicated judicial legacy to the high court.

She joined a court that had been taking a low profile, shifting to the conservative and hearing fewer cases. It had been dominated by its conservative wing—Chief Justice William Rehnquist, Clarence Thomas and Antonin Scalia. John Paul Stevens and Harry Blackmun are regarded as liberal. In the middle have been Sandra Day O'Connor, Anthony Kennedy and David Souter.

When the court opened its fall term in October 1993, Ginsburg was expected to be a moderate-to-liberal voice—certainly more liberal than Byron White.

The court's docket wasn't a very exciting one. In fact, many court observers described it as boring.

But there were some cases in the areas where Ginsburg has made her reputation. The court will consider whether abortion clinics can use federal laws against racketeering to stop protests by abortion foes. It will also consider if victims of sexual harassment have to prove they have been psychologically harmed, and whether the state can remove all men or all women from juries.

Other major cases include decisions on whether redistricting violates the rights of Hispanics, and under what conditions the government can seize property from convicted drug dealers.

President Clinton said he believed Ginsburg would be "a great justice" who would "move the court not left or right, but forward." Given her moderate judicial record, it seems the president has made, in the words of Senator Joseph Biden, a "wise and insightful" choice.

Glossary

Abortion: Expulsion of a human fetus during the first 12 weeks of gestation.

Affirmative Action: An active effort to improve the employment or educational opportunities of members of minority groups and women.

Attorney General: The chief law officer of a nation or state who represents the government in litigation and serves as its principal legal adviser.

Civil Rights: The rights of personal liberty guaranteed to U.S. citizens by the 13th and the 14th amendments to the Constitution.

Confirmation: The ceremony of admitting a person to full membership of an organization or governing body.

Congress: The lawmaking body of the United States of America.

Conservative: Someone who adheres to traditional methods or views.

Constitution: The fundamental law of a state which guides and limits the use of power by the government.

Debate: A formal discussion or argument.

Democrat: A member of the Democratic Party.

Executive: A person, group, or branch of government that has the duty and power of putting laws into effect.

Gavel: A small wooden hammer used in a meeting or in court to signal for attention or order.

Gender: The sex of an individual.

Independent: A person not associated with any established political party.

Judicial: Having something to do with a court of law or the administration of justice.

Justice: A judge, especially on the Supreme Court.

Liberal: Someone who is not strict in the observance of traditional methods or views.

Marshal: An officer of various kinds, especially a police officer.

Media: The means of mass communication such as newspapers, magazines, radio, and television.

Nomination: Naming a political candidate for office.

Political Parties: Political organizations, such as the Democratic and Republican parties.

Prejudice: An opinion formed against a person without taking time and care to judge fairly.

Radical: Favoring extreme changes or reforms.

Republican: A member of the Republican Party.

Senate: A governing or lawmaking assembly.

Tenure: The act, right, manner, or term of holding something, such as a teaching position.

United States Court of Appeals: A court hearing appeals from the decisions of lower courts.

United States Supreme Court: The highest court in the United States, which meets in Washington, D.C. It consists of eight associate justices and one chief justice.

Waiver: The act of intentionally giving up a known right, claim, or privilege.

Index